**BLASTOFF!**
**MR JONES Goes To Jupiter**
**By Jim Parker and Tom Stanier**

## ACT 1

*The musical begins with two announcements over the PA system:*
FIRST ANNOUNCEMENT *(one minute before curtain up):*
Mission Control to School Hall. Mission Control calling School Hall.
Countdown beginning in one minute. Kindly take your seats and stand by for Blastoff.

SECOND ANNOUNCEMENT *(ten seconds before curtain up):*
Mission Control to School Hall. Stand by for Blastoff. *(The audience should be encouraged to join in the countdown. Jog them into action by planting members of the cast at the back of the hall).* Countdown beginning:
10. . . 9. . . 8. . . 7. . . 6. . . 5. . . 4. . . 3. . . 2. . . 1. . . BLASTOFF!

### Scene 1

*On* 'BLASTOFF' — *the* MUSIC No.1 — OVERTURE *begins. The curtain rises on an empty office. The phone is ringing.* MRS TAYLOR, *the School Secretary, enters. She is carrying the morning post. She picks up the phone.*

MRS TAYLOR: Yes. . . yes. . . yes. . . well, *blow* the dinner money! *(Replaces receiver and starts opening the post.)* What have we got today? School Medical Officer. . . PTA circular. . . job application. Boring, boring, boring! *(She sees a letter that makes her sit up.)* Hullo. The Education Office. "Dear Headmaster, in view of the education cuts we have had to take a hard critical look at the future of your school. . . blah, blah, blah. . . We feel bound to point out that your own performance in recent months leaves something to be desired." Ooh, nasty!

GLADYS, MAVIS *and* DORIS *enter brandishing mops.*

DORIS: Morning, Mrs Taylor.

MRS TAYLOR: Hullo, Doris.

DORIS: We've come about the mops.

MRS TAYLOR: Hang on a mo. Let me just do my filing. One thing at a time. Got to be businesslike in my job. *(She takes the letters over to the waste paper basket and throws them in.)* Right, what is it then?

GLADYS: It's the mops, innit.

MRS TAYLOR: What about them?

MAVIS: They're a disgrace, that's what. Look at the head on this. *(Points mop at her)* Bald as a coot.

MRS TAYLOR: See what you mean.

DORIS: Me and the other girls want to register a complaint. Isn't that right, girls? *(They all nod vigorously.)*

MAVIS: 'fficial complaint.

GLADYS: 'fficial.

MRS TAYLOR: Mr Jones said he'd order some more last term.

DORIS: But he didn't, did he?

MRS TAYLOR: No. He's been a bit funny these last few weeks. A bit preoccupied like.

GLADYS: What's going on?

MRS TAYLOR: Blowed if I know. Tell you what. Come back in twenty minutes. He should be free then.

*As they exit the phone rings.*

MRS TAYLOR: Hullo, Snodbury Middle School. . . who's that? Oh, yes, *The Clarion.* Can I help you? . . . Have we built a what? . . . an eighty foot high spaceship? Hang on, I'll go and ask the headmaster. *(She presses the intercom switch.)* Mr Jones, it's *The Clarion.* They want to know if we've built an eighty foot high spaceship. (MR JONES's *voice comes back totally inaudible. She picks up the phone again to talk to The Clarion).* Yes, they have built one. . . When's it being launched? *(To* MR JONES) When's it being launched? *(More inaudible noises on the intercom.)* He says this afternoon at 2.15. . . not at all. Oh, and if you're doing a piece, my name's Mrs Taylor. I've been school secretary for 29 years, and I've a very nice cocker spaniel called Susie. Pleasure to be of assistance. *(Replaces receiver and hangs coat up.)* Eighty foot high spaceship. I don't know. Nobody tells me anything in this place.

MR JONES *enters dressed as a spaceman.*

MRS TAYLOR: Mr Jones! Where do you think you're going?

MR JONES: To the planets, Mrs Taylor, to the stars!

MRS TAYLOR: Eh?

MR JONES: To a better world, where there are no more leaking roofs, no more Education committees, and no more spending cuts.

MRS TAYLOR: You can't go to space.

MR JONES: Why not?

MRS TAYLOR: Because you haven't done last week's dinner money.

MR JONES: Pah!

MRS TAYLOR: Well, you haven't, have you? And anyway, where is this spaceship of yours?

MR JONES: Look through the window.

*She looks out.*

MRS TAYLOR: Blimey! Who made it?

MR JONES *(calling out to the back of the hall):* *Who made it?*

CHILDREN: *We did!*

*The* CHILDREN *march up through the hall dressed as spacemen and singing their space song. They are accompanied by a mob of their friends who have come to see them off.*

MUSIC No. 2 — LET'S GO TO THE PLANETS

SPACE CREW *and* FRIENDS *(sing):*

Let's go to the planets,
Let's go to the stars.
Let's journey to Jupiter,
Let's journey to Mars.
Let's go to the universe,
Let's search and explore,
For a thousand stars are waiting,
A thousand stars and more.

Sail through the heavens,
Through the ocean of night,
Where the planets turn
And the meteors burn
And the Milky Way shines bright.
Sail through the heavens,
Through the universe wide.
We will journey far
With the brightest star
As our beacon and our guide.

Let's go to the planets,
Let's go to the stars.
Let's journey to Jupiter,
Let's journey to Mars.
Let's go to the universe,
Let's search and explore,
For a thousand stars are waiting,
A thousand stars and more.

MRS TAYLOR: All right, who did it? Who's responsible for this thing?

CHILDREN: The Professor.

MR JONES: Show her the plans, Peter.

THE PROFESSOR, *a studious-looking boy, unrolls the plans in the shape of an enormously long computer print-out. His explanation baffles everyone, including* MRS TAYLOR.

PROFESSOR: Well, basically it's very simple. It was just a question of getting the formula sorted out. As you will observe, the turbo pump is next to the heat exchanger, which of course improves the performance of the oxidiser, and maximises the cryogenic fuel tanks. Simple isn't it?

MRS TAYLOR: Er yes . . . very nice, Peter. (*To* MR JONES) But I still say it's ridiculous.

MR JONES: Why?

MRS TAYLOR: Come here. *(Beckons him into office)* Face facts, Mr Jones. You'll never make an astronaut.

MR JONES: Why not?

MRS TAYLOR: Well, look at you. You're the middle-aged headmaster of a middle-aged school and you're about to be closed down.

MR JONES: Defeatist talk.

MRS TAYLOR: It's not on, Mr Jones. You've got fallen arches and falling rolls (*slaps* MR JONES's *wrist as he absent-mindedly takes a biscuit from a plate*) And no biscuits for you. You're putting on much too much weight.

MR JONES: What you don't seem to realise, Mrs Taylor, is that we are going to put this school on the map.

MRS TAYLOR: Hmph!

MR JONES: You wait, once we're up in space we'll be headline news, and then we'll see what the Education Committee has to say. They won't *dare* to close us down.

MRS TAYLOR: That's as may be. But what about today's engagements? *(Opens diary)* Two o'clock . . . delegation of cleaning ladies.

MR JONES: Tell them I'm on a school trip.

MRS TAYLOR: Then there's the caretaker. He's coming about the drains.

MR JONES: Tell him . . . I'm rolling back the frontiers of human knowledge.

MRS TAYLOR: What about the Inspector?

MR JONES: The dreaded Huggins! Tell Miss Huggins it's one small step for Snodbury Middle School, but a giant step for mankind. *(Resolutely)* And now we must be off. Do we have our life support system?

CHILDREN: Yes.

MR JONES: Do we have our oxygen bottles?

CHILDREN: Yes.

MR JONES: Do we have our sandwiches?

CHILDREN: Yes.

MR JONES: All systems go. Here is your walkie-talkie and computer, Mrs Taylor. From now on you are not just a School Secretary, you are Mission Control.

MRS TAYLOR *(suddenly interested)*: Mmm!

MR JONES: These are the controls — power, ignition, the lot. And when you hear the word 'Blastoff' you will kindly press this button here and blast us off into space.

MRS TAYLOR: Ooh nice!

MR JONES: Right, all aboard!

MR JONES *leads his crew off-stage, the rest of the* CHILDREN *give encouraging cheers.*

CHILD SPECTATORS: Good luck Snodbury! See you next term, Mr Jones.

GLADYS, MAVIS *and* DORIS *re-enter the office.*

DORIS: Well here we are. Mr Jones back yet?

MRS TAYLOR: Sorry, girls. He's gone off on a school trip.

DORIS: School trip? Have you heard about this, Gladys?

GLADYS: No, Doris.

*Enter* CARETAKER

CARETAKER: Afternoon. Come about the drains. Where's Mr Jones?

MRS TAYLOR: He's tied up. Rolling back the frontiers of human knowledge.

CARETAKER, GLADYS, MAVIS *and* DORIS: He's what?

MISS HUGGINS, *the Inspector, enters.*

MRS TAYLOR: Oh hullo, Miss Huggins.

MISS HUGGINS: A word with the headmaster please. Important business. Can't wait.

MRS TAYLOR: Ah, I'm to tell you, it's one small Middle for Snodbury Step School . . . No, that's wrong. It's one small Snodbury for Middle Step School . . . Oh bother! Well, you can't see him anyway.

MISS HUGGINS: Why not?

MRS TAYLOR: Have a look out of the window.

*As they crowd to the window,* MRS TAYLOR *dons a Mission Control hat, and concentrates on the intercom.*

CARETAKER: Blimey!

MR JONES'S *voice is heard from off-stage, distorted through a microphone.*

MR JONES: Starship Snodbury to Mission Control. Do you read me?

MRS TAYLOR: Mission Control standing by.

MR JONES: Thirty seconds to take-off.

DORIS: What's he playing at?

GLADYS: No wonder they want to close him down.

MR JONES: Stand by for countdown.

MAVIS: What about our mops?

MRS TAYLOR: Quiet, girls. It's my big moment. (*To* MR JONES) All systems operational.

MR JONES: Countdown beginning!

MUSIC No. 3 — BLASTOFF!

MR JONES: Ten. . .

MRS TAYLOR *(softer)*: . . .Ten

All *(sing)*: Now is the hour.

MR JONES: Nine. . .

MRS TAYLOR: . . .Nine

ALL: Activate power.

MR JONES: Eight. . .

MRS TAYLOR: . . .Eight

ALL: Check the ignition.

MR JONES: Seven. . .

MRS TAYLOR: . . .Seven

ALL: Starting the mission.

MR JONES: Six. . .

MRS TAYLOR: . . .Six

ALL: Switch on the unit.

MR JONES: Five. . .

MRS TAYLOR: . . .Five

ALL: Check it and tune it.

MR JONES: Four. . .

MRS TAYLOR: . . .Four

ALL: Taking the brake off.

MR JONES: Three. . .

MRS TAYLOR: . . .Three

ALL: Seconds to take-off.

MR JONES: Two. . .

MRS TAYLOR: . . .Two

ALL: Everyone ready? Ready . . . steady . . . Blastoff!

MRS TAYLOR: Blastoff!

*There is a pathetically feeble sound, like that of a car trying to start with a flat battery. Then silence. The subsequent silence is broken by* MR JONES's *voice on the walkie-talkie.*

MR JONES: Mrs Taylor!

MRS TAYLOR: Yes.

MR JONES: Did you remember to press the button?

MRS TAYLOR: Oh no, silly me!

MR JONES: Very well, we will start the countdown again. Not a good start, Mrs Taylor.

MRS TAYLOR: Sorry, Mr Jones.

MR JONES: Standby for countdown.

MISS HUGGINS: I'm bound to say that this is all highly irregular.

MRS TAYLOR: Shut up. I'm concentrating.

MUSIC No. 4 — BLASTOFF! *(Reprise)*
*The song is repeated. This time there is the sound of a rocket taking off on the word 'Blastoff'. The eyes of the children spectators on stage follow the rocket upwards, and their faces are lit by a red light, as if from the rocket's flame. Meanwhile the final phrase with the words 'Blastoff' is repeated ad lib with everyone joining in. There are scenes of jubilation on stage and* GLADYS, MAVIS *and* DORIS *do a little dance routine with their mops. At the end of the song there is a quick blackout to allow the astronaut crew to take their positions on the stage spaceship.*

**Scene 2**

*Fade up lights on the interior of the spaceship. The crew are all sitting up tensely in their seats shaking with the vibration of the rocket and with their eyes shut. As the rocket leaves the earth's atmosphere they stop shaking and begin to open their eyes.*

PROFESSOR: Crikey, we've made it!

LINDA: Course we have. You said it would work, didn't you.

PROFESSOR *(doubtfully)*: Oh yes, so I did.

LINDA *(waking up the others)*: Come on, we're up. We've done it.

JIMMY: Have we got there yet?

LINDA: No idea. Where are we going, Prof?

PROFESSOR: Haven't a clue. Better ask Mr Jones.

MR JONES *is still sitting rigidly in his seat with his eyes tightly shut.*

PROFESSOR: Sir.

MR JONES: What? Why are you children out of school?

LINDA: We're on a space trip, sir.

MR JONES: Good Heavens! So we are.

SALLY: What do we do now, sir?

MR JONES: What do we do now?

SALLY: Yes, what next?

MR JONES: I'll tell you what we do next. We roll back the frontiers of knowledge.

JIMMY: Yes, we know all that, but where exactly are we going?

MR JONES: Ah, the secret can now be revealed. *(Takes piece of paper out of pocket and consults it)* Our destination is none other than the planet Jupiter.

ALL: Wow! Jupiter!

MR JONES: Yes, fellow astronauts, we will be the first humans ever to set foot on that planet. Think of that. History will be made. And now I would like to propose a vote of thanks to the Professor for the successful launch of Starship Snodbury *(applause)* . . . And to celebrate the successful conclusion of stage one, I suggest that we all have something to eat. *(Cheers)* So get your sandwiches out.

GEORGE: Er, we already have, sir.

MR JONES: What?

GEORGE: While Mrs Taylor was trying to get the rocket started.

SALLY: Yes, we thought it might be a long wait.

LINDA: And some of us got a bit hungry.

MR JONES: So you ate them. Very well, no matter. We will break open the Starship's provisions. Who's in charge of the food?

GEORGE: I am, sir.

MR JONES: Good boy, George. And what have you got for us?

GEORGE: Three thousand pork pies, and five hundred tins of baked beans.

MR JONES: And?

GEORGE: That's it.

SALLY: What else did you bring?

GEORGE: Nothing.

ALL: Nothing!

GEORGE: Except for the tomato ketchup *(pause)* . . . four hundred bottles.

MR JONES *(consulting his notes)*: Let me get this straight. Three thousand pork pies, five hundred tins of baked beans and four hundred bottles of tomato sauce?

GEORGE: That's it.

SALLY: Honestly, George! What do we do with three thousand pork pies?

GEORGE: Well, I like them.

MR JONES: Never mind. It's not the end of the world. Let's think of what lies ahead of us.

PROFESSOR: We are.

JIMMY: Five hunded tins of baked beans.

POLLY: And three months in a spaceship.

MR JONES: Not the best of planning, I grant you.

PROFESSOR: The atmosphere may build up.

SALLY: You can say that again!

JIMMY: And what about all that ketchup? What's the point of that, George?

GEORGE: Well, it's a space trip, isn't it? You can't be a proper spaceman without the sauce.

JIMMY: Eh?

GEORGE: Like in *Star Wars.* The Sauce is with us, the Sauce is with us always.

LINDA: Force, you dummy! Not sauce . . . *Force!*

ALL: Oh, George! You wally!

MR JONES: The Force? *Star Wars?*

PROFESSOR: You know, Luke Skywalker.

JIMMY: Darth Vader.

POLLY: Princess Leia.

MR JONES: I see. Well, enough of this foolish chit-chat. We are not taking part in some clapped-out Hollywood soap opera. Starship Snodbury is for real. And don't look so gloomy, my friends: we are each of us intergalactic superstars. What are we?

ALL *(gloomily)*: Intergalactic superstars.

GEORGE: Sorry about the sauce, sir.

MR JONES: Nothing to be sorry about, George. Hand it round, hand it round. (GEORGE *hands out bottles of ketchup to the crew.*) Heads high, my friends. We too will venture boldly where no man has gone before. And who knows? The Sauce could yet prove to be our secret weapon. Anything *Star Wars* can do, we can do better.

MUSIC No. 5 — THE SAUCE IS WITH US

All *(sing)*:

*Hold high the Sauce,*
*A product we endorse,*
*The Sauce will be with us always.*
*Who wants the Force*
*When you have got the Sauce?*
*The Sauce will be with us always.*
*The Sauce, the Sauce, the Sauce for every course!*
*The Sauce will be with us always!*

MR JONES *(sings)*: Let each man hold his head high,
And be a space crusader.
We'll fight them like the Jedi,
And grapple with Darth Vader.
The mission we must see to
Does not need R2D2.
The Sauce will be with us always.

ALL: *Hold high the Sauce, etc*

MR JONES: We may lack Princess Leia
And boring old Skywalker.
But there's no need to fear,
Our spaceship is a corker.
Our spaceship is a cracker.
If aliens attack her,
The Sauce is with us always.

ALL: *Hold high the Sauce, etc*

MR JONES: Bravo, boys and girls. Onward to the stars! Onward to the planets! Onward to Jupiter!

*(Cheers)*

JIMMY: Just one question, sir. How do we know where Jupiter is?

MR JONES: Simple. We get the maps out. Who's got them? *(Silence)* Come on, who's in charge of the space charts?

PROFESSOR: I think you said you'd bring them.

MR JONES: Nonsense.

LINDA: You did, sir.

MR JONES: Oh no, I didn't.

ALL: Oh yes, you did.

MR JONES: Oh no, I didn't.

ALL: Oh yes, you did.

MR JONES: This is getting silly. Only one way to settle it. Get me Mission Control. (LINDA *fiddles with some switches and passes a mike to* MR JONES.) This is Starship Snodbury. Come in, Mrs Taylor. Are you receiving me?

*Fade up spot on* MRS TAYLOR'*s office with* MRS TAYLOR *doing her knitting.*

MRS TAYLOR: Oh hullo, Mr Jones. How's it going?

MR JONES: Fine, Mrs Taylor, fine. Everything's under control.

MRS TAYLOR: Oh good.

MR JONES: Just one thing. You remember those space charts?

MRS TAYLOR: Yes, lovely they were. Ever so smart.

MR JONES: Which child picked them up from the office?

MRS TAYLOR: Which child? Oh no. Don't you remember? You told me to keep them handy till take-off. Said they'd be safer that way.

MR JONES: You mean you've got them?

MRS TAYLOR: Course I have. *(Rummages in her knitting basket)* Here they are. Don't you worry, Mr Jones. They're nice and safe in my knitting basket.

MR JONES *(slumping in his seat)*: Over and out. They're in her knitting basket!

SALLY: Cheer up, sir, it's not the end of the world.

MR JONES: Isn't it? The whole expedition's ruined, and it's all my fault. I'm a failure, a total failure. Everything I touch is disaster.

PROFESSOR: Maybe we can come up with something. Let's have a whip-round. Anyone got anything?

JIMMY: I've got a pocket compass.

GEORGE: And I've got a map of the underground. This any good, sir?

MR JONES: Well, it depends, doesn't it? Have they extended the Central Line to Jupiter? *(Looks at underground map)* No, I thought not. Starship Snodbury is doomed.

LINDA: Hang on a minute. There's something coming.

PROFESSOR: What is it?

LINDA: It's some sort of flying object.

PROFESSOR: Can you identify it?

LINDA: Never seen anything quite like it.

PROFESSOR: Aha. An unidentified flying object.

ALL: A U.F.O.

PROFESSOR: Precisely.

*During the preceding remarks the* U.F.O. *has advanced from the back of the hall. It arrives at the rocket and talks through the window.*

UFO: Good-day to you. Can I come in?

SALLY: There's a door at the back. Through the airlock.

UFO *enters rocket.*

JIMMY: Come on, sir. There's a U.F.O. to see you.

MR JONES: Who? My goodness! Well I never!

UFO: Good afternoon.

MR JONES: Er, how do you do?

UFO: Just passing through. Thought I'd drop in for a spot of civilised conversation.

MR JONES: Fine. Well, let me introduce ourselves. I'm Mr Jones, and this is Linda, Peter, Polly, Sally, Jimmy and George.

UFO: Very pleased to meet you. Mr Furtzlebanger says it's good for me to meet young people.

MR JONES: Who's Mr Furtzlebanger?

UFO: My psychiatrist.

MR JONES: Oh, really?

UFO: Yes, I pop in for check-ups every 500 years.

MR JONES: Look, excuse my asking, but who exactly are you?

UFO: You don't know?

MR JONES: No.

UFO: You're sure?

MR JONES: I'm afraid not.

UFO: Absolutely certain?

MR JONES: Yes, I'm very sorry, but I really don't think I've had the pleasure.

*The* U.F.O. *throws a hysterical fit and then abruptly recovers.*

UFO: Ah well, it was only to be expected.

MR JONES: What was?

UFO: It's the same old story. Identity crisis. You don't know who I am. Nobody knows who I am. Even I don't know who I am. It's so depressing.

MR JONES: It can't be as bad as all that.

UFO: Oh, can't it? Furtzlebanger says I'm the biggest fruit-cake in the Solar System.

POLLY *(turning to others)*: What's he on about?

UFO: I'll tell you what I'm on about. Listen.

MUSIC No. 6 — U.F.O. BLUES

UFO *(sings)*:

I'm a U.F.O., and not too clear
As to why exactly I am here.
Who can I be?
Why am I me?
It's so hard to know
For a U.F.O.,
Oh, oh, I don't know,
I'm an unidentifiable U.F.O.

SPACE CREW *(sing)*: *Oh, oh, I don't know,*
*He's an unidentifiable U.F.O.*

UFO: I'm a U.F.O., and rather fear
My identity is not too clear.
Am I a Paul,
Simon or Saul?
It's so hard to know
For a U.F.O.
Oh, oh, I don't know,
I'm an unidentifiable U.F.O.

SPACE CREW: *Oh, oh, I don't know,*
*He's an unidentifiable U.F.O.*

UFO: I'm a U.F.O., and must confess
Psychologically I'm in a mess.
My neurosis slowly grows —
I'm the U.F.O. that no one knows.
Oh, oh, I don't know,
I'm an unidentifiable U.F.O.

SPACE CREW: *Oh, oh, I don't know,*
*He's an unidentifiable U.F.O.*

UFO: It is undeniable
I'm an unreliable
Unidentifiable
U...F...O....

SPACE CREW: *It is undeniable*
*He's an unreliable*
*Unidentifiable*
*U...F...O....*

UFO: Did you find that interesting?

MR JONES *(without much conviction)*: Oh yes, very.

UFO: In that case I'll tell you the rest of my medical history. You'll enjoy that.

MR JONES *(doubtfully)*: Er...yes.

UFO: Not often I get someone to talk to these days. *(Warming to his task)* You see, what's so remarkable is that Furtzlebanger thinks I'm a classic case. He says my endogenous depression is coupled with doubts about my ego potency, and recently I've shown clear signs of mid-life rocket envy. You follow?

MR JONES *(starting to nod off)*: Er...mm.

UFO: Another thing Furtzlebanger points out is that I'm incredibly boring. That's why he only sees me once every 500 years. Do you find me boring? (*Pokes sleeping* MR JONES) I said, do you find me boring?

MR JONES *(waking up)*: No, no, not at all. Fascinating account. Wake up, children.

UFO: Still, I mustn't talk about my problems the whole time. Let's talk about yours.

MR JONES: Ah, so you know about the missing charts?

UFO: Charts? I don't know anything about that? I'm talking about the Black Hole.

ALL: Black Hole!

UFO: Didn't you know? You're heading straight for one of the most unpleasant Black Holes in the universe.

ALL: What!

UFO: Oh yes. Very nasty indeed. Last year it ate fourteen stars, twelve asteroids and three multi-channel weather satellites. I strongly advise you to alter course.

JIMMY: Quick, sir, let's get out of it.

MR JONES: Not so fast I feel the call of the unknown.

LINDA: Oh, no!

MR JONES: This could be our chance to go boldly where no man has gone before. I've always wanted to meet a Black Hole.

LINDA: I haven't.

UFO: I must warn you that if you go too close you will be sucked inside and squashed to the size of a cigarette lighter.

ALL: Eek!

UFO: You could of course make an important scientific discovery at the same time.

GEORGE: I never did like science.

UFO: Up to you. Do you still want to meet it?

MR JONES: Yes.

CHILDREN: No.

MR JONES: Yes.

CHILDREN: No.

UFO: Well, you'd better make your mind up soon because here it comes.

*The* BLACK HOLE *appears at the back of the hall to spooky tone-clusters low down on the piano.*

BLACK HOLE: Good evening, revolting Earthlings. You may boo if you wish because I am extremely villainous. (CAST, *encouraging* AUDIENCE, *boo vigorously*) Thank you. Why am I so villainous? Allow me to tell you in detail.

*During the course of the song the* BLACK HOLE *wanders among the audience making threatening noises, and at the end of the song it advances towards the rocket.*

MUSIC No. 7 — THE BLACK HOLE SONG

BLACK HOLE *(sings)*:

I'm black as night,
I squeeze you tight,
I'm a Black, Black, Black Hole.
I squeeze you flat
To the size of a gnat,
I'm a Black, Black, Black Hole
I can seize you,
I can squeeze you,
In a way that's not designed to please you.
You'll disappear
If you come too near
To a Black, Black, Black Hole.

We're rarely seen,
We're evil and mean,
We're the Black, Black, Black Holes.
We're rated low
As aperatures go,
We're the Black, Black, Black Holes.
If we meet you,
We will eat you,
In a word, we're likely to delete you.
The course to steer
Is not too clear
To a Black, Black, Black Hole.

You can't do much
To escape the clutch
Of a Black, Black, Black Hole.
You can scream and shout
But you can't get out
Of a Black, Black, Black Hole.
We're the Black Holes,
We're the Black Holes,
We're the ultimate in cul-de-sac holes.
You're out of luck
If you find you're stuck
In a Black, Black, Black Hole.
We're the dreaded Black Holes,
Nasty cul-de-sac holes,
Black. . .
Black. . .
Black. . .
Holes.

BLACK HOLE: Well, well, well, what have we here? Looks like my dinner. Haven't had a nice tasty spaceship for a long time.

MR JONES: Stand back, boys. This one's for me.

BLACK HOLE: Are you coming out, or do I have to come in and get you?

MR JONES: I'm not scared of you, you great bully.

BLACK HOLE: Go on, make my day.

MR JONES: Watch this boys. Notice the way I dominate him with the force of my personality.

MR JONES *leaves the spaceship.*

UFO: Are you sure you know what you're doing?

MR JONES: Now look here. I'll have you know that I'm the headmaster of Snodbury Middle School.

BLACK HOLE: Oh yeah?

MR JONES: And I'm not going to stand any nonsense from you.

BLACK HOLE: Is that so?

MR JONES *is pulled towards the* BLACK HOLE.

MR JONES: Do you hear me? I won't stand for it. I won't stand for it.

MR JONES *is sucked inside the* BLACK HOLE. *There is a slurping/belching sort of noise and a tin of corned beef is ejected.*

BLACK HOLE: Gordon Bennett. That was quite disgusting. These schoolmasters. They're all the same — tough as old boots. I really must stick to astronauts.

MUSIC No. 8 — BLACK HOLE (*Reprise*)

BLACK HOLE *(sings)*:

You can't do much
To escape the clutch
Of a Black, Black, Black Hole.
You can scream and shout
But you can't get out
Of a Black, Black, Black Hole.
We're the Black Holes,
We're the Black Holes,
We're the ultimate in cul-de-sac holes.
You're out of luck
If you find you're stuck
In a Black, Black, Black Hole.
We're the dreaded Black Holes,
Nasty cul-de-sac holes,
Black . . .
Black . . .
Black . . .
Holes.

*Exit* BLACK HOLE.

UFO: Oh dear, oh dear, oh dear. I'd better go and pick him up — what's left of him.

PROFESSOR: Crikey.

JIMMY: What do we do now?

LINDA: Dunno.

*The* UFO *re-enters carrying the tin of corned beef.*

UFO: Here you are. Who wants him? Any takers?

GEORGE: Is that Mr Jones?

PROFESSOR: Not the man he was, is he?

POLLY: What's happened to him?

UFO: He has gone boldly where no man went before.

*The phone rings inside the spaceship.*

SALLY: What's that?

PROFESSOR: Go on, answer it.

*Fade up spot on* MRS TAYLOR *at her switchboard.*

MRS TAYLOR: Mission control calling. This is mission control.

SALLY: Who's that?

MRS TAYLOR: You know . . . it's me, Mrs Taylor. Is that you, Sally?

SALLY: Yes.

MRS TAYLOR: How's it going, dear? Anything happened yet?

SALLY: We've met up with a U.F.O.

MRS TAYLOR: Really?

SALLY: And we've just bumped into a Black Hole.

MRS TAYLOR: Black Hole? Well, fancy that. These school trips are marvellous. Now can I have a word with Mr Jones?

SALLY (*holding the corned beef*): Er no, I'm afraid you can't.

MRS TAYLOR: Why not?

SALLY: He's not available at the moment.

MRS TAYLOR: Oh, I understand.

JIMMY: No you don't.

MRS TAYLOR: Well, it's not important. I just wanted to tell him that the local press is coming round to interview me. How is he anyway?

SALLY: Mr Jones?

MRS TAYLOR: Yes.

SALLY: Well, he's lost a lot of weight.

MRS TAYLOR: Oh good, just what he needed.

*There is a knock on the door and* CLAYTON *of THE CLARION appears, a local journalist of a somewhat clapped-out nature.*

MRS TAYLOR: Well, I must be going now. (*Stage whisper*) It's the media. Bye.

*Fade out spot on spaceship.*

CLAYTON: Mrs Taylor?

MRS TAYLOR: Yes.

CLAYTON: I'm Clayton. *Snodbury Clarion.* We spoke on the phone.

MRS TAYLOR: Oh, yes. Pleased to meet you, Mr Clayton. Have a seat.

CLAYTON: My editor told me to pop in. Asked me to see how the spaceship's getting on.

MRS TAYLOR: Oh, yes. Well, everything's going very nicely.

CLAYTON: But nothing much to report?

MRS TAYLOR: Not really.

CLAYTON: That's what I said to my editor. Non-story, I said.

MRS TAYLOR: Let me see, they've had a U.F.O. on board.

CLAYTON (*taking notes*): U.F.O. . . .

MRS TAYLOR: And they've just bumped into a Black Hole.

CLAYTON: Black Hole . . . Mm. That's it, is it?

MRS TAYLOR: That's it. No real surprises.

CLAYTON: Just as I thought. Non-story. I've got a nose of these things, you know. Infallible. (*Taps the side of his nose knowledgeably*)

MRS TAYLOR: I'm sure. Cup of tea?

CLAYTON: Thank you. (MRS TAYLOR *pours the tea while* CLAYTON *rambles on.*) That's the trouble with working on a local paper. We've got the talent; we've got the news sense; but somehow we just don't seem to get the stories. Take this Starship thing. I'd give it ten lines on page four. That's all it's worth. Ten lines.

MRS TAYLOR: Really? I think it's wonderful the way you know these things.

CLAYTON: Judgement and experience. Priceless commodities, Mrs Taylor, and Clayton of *The Clarion* has them in abundance. A very nice drop of tea if I may say so.

MRS TAYLOR: Thank you.

CLAYTON: Now tell me a bit more about your cocker spaniel.

MRS TAYLOR: Susie? Oh, she's lovely. You have one too, do you?

CLAYTON: Indeed I have.

MRS TAYLOR: Well, a man with your nose will appreciate this. My Susie has won first prize twice running at the Snodbury Dog Show.

CLAYTON: No!

MRS TAYLOR: Yes.

CLAYTON: There's your story, Mrs Taylor. Take it from me; There's your story (*taps side of nose*). Infallible.

*Blackout.* MRS TAYLOR *and* CLAYTON *leave the stage. Fade up lights again on spaceship.*

**Scene 3**

*Back on the spaceship.*

LINDA: Well, what do we do now?

UFO: Might I ask a question? What were you doing up here anyway?

PROFESSOR: We were off to Jupiter.

UFO: What for?

POLLY: To get some Jupiter rock.

UFO: Was that one of Mr Jones's ideas?

SALLY: Yes.

UFO: I though it might have been.

GEORGE: What's wrong with it?

UFO: Jupiter's made of gas.

PROFESSOR: So what?

UFO: There aren't any rocks on Jupiter.

GEORGE: Oh.

UFO: May I ask another question? Do you want Mr Jones back?

SALLY: Yes, of course we do . . . well, I think so.

LINDA: Do we? (*Pause*)

PROFESSOR: Yes, I suppose we do. (*Pause*)

POLLY: On the other hand . . .

JIMMY: Come on. Of course we want him back. He's got my compass.

GEORGE: Poor old geezer. Don't be so rotten to him.

SALLY: All right. Yes, we do want him back.

UFO: Well, in that case, why don't you look for a White Hole?

ALL: A White Hole?

ALL *look at each other blankly.*

LINDA: Excuse my asking, but what exactly is a White Hole?

UFO: It's perfectly simple. A Black Hole makes you shrink, and a White Hole makes you expand. (*Pause*) Well, it's obvious, isn't it? If you put Mr Jones in a White Hole, you'll get your headmaster back.

JIMMY: Crikey, that's good.

SALLY: Brilliant! Let's go.

POLLY: Yes, where are the White Holes?

UFO: Ah, that poses a slight problem. I don't know where they are.

PROFESSOR (*sarcastically*): Terrific.

UFO: But you will be able to find the answer if you go to Mars. The Aliens will guide you. And now if you will excuse me, I have a rendezvous with Furtzlebanger. Good luck with your mission.

CHILDREN: Goodbye.

UFO (*Exit, singing*): Oh, oh, I don't know,
I'm an unidentifiable U.F.O.

PROFESSOR: Well. (*Pause*)

POLLY: I don't know about you lot, but I'm getting fed up with all this.

JIMMY: Me too. I don't want to go to Mars. I want to go home.

GEORGE: Oy! We can't leave Mr Jones like this.

JIMMY: I don't believe in these White Holes.

POLLY: And I don't go for this Mars idea.

LINDA: Me neither. I mean, what reason have we got to think we'll ever get there?

*A voice appears to emerge from the corned beef.*

MR JONES: Because the sauce is with you, Linda.

LINDA: Who said that?

MR JONES: I did.

LINDA: Who's that?

MR JONES: Obi Ben Jones.

PROFESSOR: Blimey.

MR JONES: Go to Mars, children, go to Mars. The Sauce is with you.

GEORGE: Do you hear that? The Sauce is with us. Don't worry, Mr Jones. We won't desert you, will we?

ALL: Never!

GEORGE: Stand by Mars! Starship Snodbury is coming. The Sauce is with us always!

*They brandish their sauce bottles while singing the song.*

MUSIC No. 9 — THE SAUCE IS WITH US (*Reprise*)

ALL (*sing*):

Hold high the sauce,
A product we endorse.
The Sauce will be with us always.
Who wants the Force
When you have got the Sauce?
The Sauce will be with us always.
The Sauce, the Sauce, the Sauce for every course,
The Sauce will be with us always!

ALL *repeat the chorus a second time, brandishing their bottles and countermarching up and down the stage. At the end of the verse everyone forms a heroic tableau. They are dauntless in the face of adversity. The Sauce is with them.*

CURTAIN

**ACT II**
**Scene 1**

*The surface of Mars.* MUSIC No. 10 *begins. The sound of a rocket approaching and the voices of the children are heard off-stage.*

POLLY: De-activate rockets.

LINDA: Rockets de-activated.

POLLY: Cut turbo-thrust.

LINDA: Turbo-thrust cut.

POLLY: Lower deflector shields.

JIMMY: Deflector shields lowered.

POLLY: Stand by for impact.

*Sound of rocket landing with much crashing and banging.*

POLLY: The sparrow has landed.

*The* CHILDREN *appear on stage exploring cautiously. There are two large bumps on the stage which they sit on, assuming they are rocks.*

LINDA: Where are we? Is it Mars?

SALLY: Dunno.

GEORGE: Er, are you quite sure it's safe?

POLLY: Course it is.

PROFESSOR (*reading notice on ground*): The planet Mars welcomes careful astronauts. It is Mars! We've made it!

SALLY: I wonder where everyone is. It looks awfully empty.

POLLY: Hey, wait a minute. Can you feel the ground shaking?

JIMMY: You're imagining it.

POLLY: No, I'm not. These rocks are moving.

*The 'rocks' they are sitting on stir into movement and rise up. They are in fact sleeping* ALIENS.

CHILDREN: Eek! Monsters!

ALIEN 1: Hey, wake up, gang. We've got company.

ALIEN 2: Suffering supernovas. What is this?

ALIEN 1: I guess it's some form of primitive life.

ALIEN 3: Wow, these are some weird creatures. Do you see their eyes? They've got *two* eyes.

ALIEN 1: Freaky, man, freaky. (*The* ALIENS *advance towards the* CHILDREN.) Hi there.

SALLY: Hullo.

ALIEN 4: Where are you guys from then?

SALLY: We're on a space mission from Earth.

ALIEN 2: Is that so? Earthlings, Zak, Earthlings.

ALIEN 1: Hey look, no offence meant, but are you guys normal? Do all earthlings look like you?

PROFESSOR: Yes, of course.

ALIEN 4: Two eyes?

PROFESSOR: Yes.

ALIENS: Wow! Too much, man! Far out!

*The* ALIENS *are unable to control their mirth at this last revelation and slap hands like an American football team.*

POLLY: And what about you? Do all Martians look like you?

ALIEN 1: Sure they do. Except they're not all as good-looking.

POLLY: Really?

ALIEN 1: Zak here is something else. He got a nomination for last year's Nose of the Universe Competition. You like it? (*Holds up* ZAK's *nose*) It's a bit special, isn't it?

POLLY: It certainly is.

ALIEN 2: Yeah, let's face it. I am one beauuuutiful alien.

ALIEN 1: In fact, we have a saying round these parts: the thing to be is a G.L.G.

LINDA: What's a G.L.G.

ALIEN 2: A G.L.G. is a good-looking guy. And here's a little number that says it all.

ALIEN 1: Says it all, Zak, says it all.

MUSIC No. 11 — GOOD-LOOKING GUYS

ALIENS (*sing*):

I'm an alien creature from outer space,
With an alien body and an alien face.
I've got sixty four alien toes,
And an extra-terrestrial, purple nose.
Alien creatures have alien arms,
And we count among our physical charms
Bright green ears and a luminous eye.
Golly, I'm a good-looking guy.

I'm an alien you-know-what
With a nose so long it ties in a knot.
Passing astronauts stop and stare
At my extra-terrestrial, sky-blue hair.
I've got alien bright red knees.
I smell just like Camembert cheese.
I'm so handsome you can't deny
That golly, I'm a good-looking guy.

We're a group of alien creatures,
We have such magnificent features,
Few can hope to equal or reach us
When it comes to looking good.
Judged by any normal criteria,
Earthlings are immensely inferior,
Lookswise we are clearly superior.
We look just like people should.

I'm an alien creature from outer space,
With an alien body and an alien face.
I've got sixty four alien toes,
And an extra-terrestrial, purple nose.
Alien creatures have alien arms,
And we count among our physical charms
Bright green ears and a luminous eye.
Golly, I'm a good-looking guy.
Golly, golly,
Aliens are jolly,
Jolly, jolly good-looking guys.
Golly, golly,
Aliens are jolly,
Jolly, jolly good-looking guys.

*Blackout. Fade up lights on office.*

**Scene 2**

*The Secretary's office.* MRS TAYLOR *is reading from a copy of the local paper.*

MRS TAYLOR: "Mrs Taylor, the lively and vivacious secretary of Snodbury Middle School, is working as Mission Control. In her spare time she and her cocker spaniel Susie are hoping to win the Golden Bone of Snodbury for the third year in succession." (*Knock on door*) Come in.

GLADYS, MAVIS *and* DORIS *enter.*

DORIS: We wanna see the Head.

MRS TAYLOR: You can't.

DORIS: Why not?

MRS TAYLOR: He's up there — in elevation.

GLADYS: What about the mops?

MRS TAYLOR: Oh, blow the mops! Here. It's all in *The Clarion*. Have a look at this.

| | |
|---|---|
| DORIS (*reading*): | "The space trip continues uneventfully. Apart from meeting a Black Hole and a U.F.O. there is little to report. Mrs Taylor, meanwhile, shows every sign of becoming the dog Wonder Woman of the 1980s." |
| MAVIS: | 'Ere. Who wrote this rubbish? |
| MRS TAYLOR (*sniffily*): | Clayton of *The Clarion*. And it's not rubbish. |
| GLADYS: | Why's it all about you then? |
| MRS TAYLOR: | Because he's got a nose. |
| GLADYS: | Course 'e's got a nose. |
| MRS TAYLOR: | A nose for a story. He thinks I have headline potential. I'm going to be a celebrity. |

MRS TAYLOR *takes out a pocket mirror and admires herself. A man from The Express enters with a copy of The Clarion.*

| | |
|---|---|
| EXPRESS MAN (*after checking the name in the paper*): | You Mrs Taylor? |
| MRS TAYLOR: | Yes. |
| EXPRESS MAN: | In here, folks. |
| DORIS: | What's all this? |
| EXPRESS MAN: | *Daily Express*. Come to do a story. |
| MRS TAYLOR: | See? I'm a superstar. |

*A woman with a cassette recorder arrives.*

| | |
|---|---|
| RADIO WOMAN: | Snodbury School? |
| MRS TAYLOR: | That's right. |
| RADIO WOMAN: | *Woman's Hour*. Be with you in a minute. Just pop in a cassette. |
| PHOTOGRAPHER: | Look this way, lady. Thank you. And again. |
| MAVIS: | What you want to photograph her for? |
| PHOTOGRAPHER: | Page 3, darling. |

*Flashy* TV MAN *arrives, grasps* MRS TAYLOR *by the hands and gazes deeply into her eyes.*

| | |
|---|---|
| TV MAN: | Mrs Taylor? *Sky at Night*. Great to meet you. Fantastic. Wonderful. I'm Julian Willoughby, well known for my fearless integrity and deeply-human reporting. |
| EXPRESS MAN: | Give it a rest, Julian. |
| TV MAN: | Camera and sound in here. |

CAMERAMAN *and* SOUND RECORDIST *enter and make for the nearest seats. While the* TV MAN *drivels on, they take out their newspapers and read.*

TV MAN (*Making it plain to all that he is in the throes of the creative process*): Yes . . . yes . . . I think I've got it. I want you, Jim . . .

CAMERAMAN: John.

TV MAN: I want you to paint a picture in light. OK? A picture in light. ! see this as a statement of man's cosmic dilemma. Mrs Taylor, alone and isolated in the confusion and mindless anarchy of her office.

MRS TAYLOR (*bridling*): I beg your pardon?

TV MAN: Beyond these walls lie the vast forces of the education committees, ready to break in and crush her to oblivion. And all this, Jim . . .

CAMERAMAN: John.

TV MAN: . . . has to be summed-up in one stunningly powerful visual image. Can you give me that?

CAMERAMAN (*still reading paper*): Sure.

TV MAN (*sizing up shots at about two inches from* MRS TAYLOR's *face*): Don't mind me, Mrs Taylor. Just forget I'm here. Oh yes, this is going to be strong television. This is going to be very strong.

SOUND RECORDIST: Strong? Personally, I prefer mine weak.

PHOTOGRAPHER: Did someone say coffee? How many coffees, lads? 1 . . . 2 . . . 3 . . . 4 . . . 5 . . . 6 cups of coffee please.

GLADYS (*offended*): What!

TV MAN: And a few little biccies. (*This time he gazes into* DORIS's *eyes*) OK? Great. Fantastic.

MRS TAYLOR: Well, go on, Doris. Get the coffee.

DORIS: Who do they think they are?

EXPRESS MAN: Who do we think we are?

GLADYS: Yes, who do you think you are?

TV MAN: We, madam, are the media men.

*As* GLADYS, MAVIS *and* DORIS *flounce out, the* MEDIA MEN *launch into their song.*

MUSIC No. 12 — THE MEDIA MEN

MEDIA PEOPLE (*sing*):

We are reporters,
We've come to snoop,
We want a story,
We want a scoop.
We want a story,
Preferably gory,
We are media men.

We are reporters,
We get intrusive,
We'd sell our grannies
For an exclusive.
We make the headlines,
We can meet the deadlines,
We are the media men.

We are the media men.
Bringing to the nation
Scandal and sensation.
We are the media men,
Quick on the draw
With a foot in the door.

We are reporters,
We take the notes,
We fake the pictures,
We fudge the quotes.
We want drama
Fit for Panorama.
We are the media men.

We are reporters,
Keen and alert.
We dig for gossip,
We dig for dirt.
Each revelation
Shakes the British Nation,
We are the media men.

We are the media men,
Nothing high-faluting',
We just put the boot in,
We are the media men,
Journalist hacks
Who can grind an axe.

We are reporters,
We get intrustive,
We'd sell our grannies
For an exclusive.
We make the headlines,
We can meet the deadlines,
We are the media men.
We are the media,
No one is seedier
Than the media
Men.

CAMERAMAN: Right, let's get on with it. Pubs open in ten minutes.

TV MAN: Now the thing to do, Mrs Taylor, is to relax. Forget about the cameras. It's just a normal little conversation between you, me and fifteen million listeners. OK? Board in.

*The switchboard rings loudly.*

SOUND RECORDIST: Hang on. I can hear something.

MRS TAYLOR (*answering the call*): No, it's not terribly convenient just now. I have the media here.

TV MAN: Mrs Taylor . . .

MRS TAYLOR: That's right. The media.

TV MAN: Mrs Taylor . . . do you mind? Be a love and get them off the line.

MRS TAYLOR: Get them off the line?

TV MAN: Yes please. We're busy people, you know. We've got deadlines to meet.

CAMERAMAN: Pubs open in eight minutes.

MRS TAYLOR: Right you are then. (*To phone*) Everything all right? You're on Mars? Well I must go. Give us a ring in a week.

TV MAN (*impatiently*): Thank you, Mrs Taylor. Thank you.

MRS TAYLOR: Sorry. (*Replaces phone*)

TV MAN: Great. Fantastic. OK, let's get this show on the road. Stand by everyone.

RADIO WOMAN: Hang on a moment. Who was that?

TV MAN: Nobody important.

RADIO WOMAN: I thought she said Mars.

MRS TAYLOR: Yes, I did.

RADIO WOMAN: You did? Who was it?

MRS TAYLOR: The spaceship.

ALL: What!

MRS TAYLOR: Starship Snodbury. It was only the kids ringing in.

EXPRESS MAN: Only the kids. Why didn't you say so?

MRS TAYLOR: He told me to get off the line.

TV MAN: Quick. Board in. Turn over. Get them back again, Mrs Taylor. This is going to be great television.

MRS TAYLOR: Oh no it isn't.

TV MAN: What do you mean?

MRS TAYLOR: I can't get them back. They only ring in once a week.

ALL: What!

TV MAN: I don't believe it. I just don't believe it.

MRS TAYLOR: It's all right, Mr Willoughby. They're fine. No need to wory about the Starship.

TV MAN: Stuff the Starship! What about my programme?

EXPRESS MAN: That's it then, Julian.

SOUND MAN: Looks like a wrap, lads.

PHOTOGRAPHER: Down to the pub?

ALL: Great idea. (*They start to exit.*)

MRS TAYLOR: Hang on. What about Susie?

RADIO WOMAN: Who the hell's Susie?

MRS TAYLOR: My dog.

RADIO WOMAN: Your dog?

MRS TAYLOR: Twice winner of the Golden Bone of Snodbury.

*The* RADIO WOMAN, *speechless, gazes at* MRS TAYLOR *for a moment.*

PHOTOGRAPHER: Pubs open in four minutes.

EXPRESS MAN: Mine's a pint. (*Exits*)

MRS TAYLOR: Well, I never. I've never been so insulted.

GLADYS, MAVIS *and* DORIS *return with the coffee.*

DORIS: Coffee up.

MRS TAYLOR: They've gone.

MAVIS: Good riddance, I say.

GLADYS: Reckon you're well out of that lot, Mrs Taylor.

MRS TAYLOR: Reckon I am. Pass the biscuits, Gladys. (*Puts her feet up on the desk*)

*Blackout*

**Scene 3**

*Back on Mars. The* ALIENS *and the* CHILDREN *are sitting around chatting.*

ALIEN 1: So you guys come from Snodbury.

CHILDREN: Yes.

ALIEN 1: Can't say I know it, but I guess Snodbury knows all about the Mars Bars.

GEORGE: Who are the Mars Bars?

ALIEN 2: Who are the Mars Bars?

ALIEN 4: You mean you haven't heard of us?

ALIEN 3: That's incredible. I mean, we're very big round these parts. Ain't that right, gang?

ALIENS: Yeah, very big.

ALIEN 4: Last night we did a gig down at the Three Craters, and they were just crazy about us.

ALIEN 3: Crazy, man, crazy!

ALIEN 2: Tomorrow night we're top of the bill at the Milky Way.

ALIEN 3: Top of the bill!

ALIEN 4: And next month it's the Pan Solar Song Contest. I tell you the Mars Bars are going all the way.

ALIEN 3: All the way, man! All the way!

ALIEN 4: What about you guys? Where are you heading?

PROFESSOR: Ah, that's a very good question.

POLLY: And we thought you might be able to help us.

ALIEN 4: You did?

JIMMY: It's our headmaster, you see. Where is he? (*The* CHILDREN *produce the tin of corned beef.*) Here he is.

ALIEN 2: This your headmaster? (*Reading label*) "Mr Corned Beef." Hi, Mr Beef.

ALIEN 3: He's not very big, is he?

LINDA: Not at the moment.

ALIEN 3: Is he on a diet?

LINDA: Sort of.

ALIEN 2: I said "Hi, Mr Beef". (*Silence*) Quiet sort of guy, isn't he?

PROFESSOR: I think we ought to explain. Last week we had an accident with a Black Hole.

ALIEN 1: Hey, bad vibes, man.

PROFESSOR: It was bad vibes for Mr Jones, all right.

LINDA: He went straight up to it. Ever so brave he was. But it just swallowed him up.

ALIEN 4: That's tough.

LINDA: Yes, that's what the Black Hole said.

ALIEN 1: So what do you want us to do?

JIMMY: Well, we met a U.F.O. . . .

ALIEN 1: Don't tell me. (*Sings*) *I'm an unidentifiable U.F.O.*

LINDA: That's the one. Do you know him?

ALIEN 3: Do we know him? Everyone knows him. He's the biggest bore in the galaxy. Right, guys?

ALIEN 4: Heavy, man, heavy.

JIMMY: Well, he said that what we needed for Mr Jones was a White Hole. Is that right?

ALIEN 1: Could be.

JIMMY: Trouble was he didn't know where the White Holes lived, but he said you lot on Mars might be able to help.

SALLY: So could you tell us where to find them, please?

ALIEN 1: What do you think, gang?

ALIENS: Why not?

ALIEN 1: OK. Who's got the A to Z?

ALIEN 3: Here it is. (*Produces large gazeteer and leafs through it*) Let's see . . . White Holes. Page 57, square 4G . . . Here we are.

POLLY: How do we get there?

ALIEN 3: Well, you could try heading for Orion.

ALIEN 4: That's the scenic route.

ALIEN 3: Take the first right after Sirius and carry on to the Crab Nebula. After that you just slip into light speed gear.

ALIEN 4: That way, you get there by yesterday. OK?

PROFESSOR: Thanks a lot. Well, we'd better be going. Could we have our headmaster back?

ALIEN 2: Sure. Best of luck. And to you, Mr Beef.

ALIEN 1: By the way, what were you guys doing up in space in the first place?

GEORGE: We were heading for Jupiter.

SALLY: To be the first people from Earth to make a landing.

POLLY: And we were going to bring back a sample of Jupiter rock. Only that wasn't a very good idea.

ALIEN 3: Why not?

PROFESSOR: Because there isn't any rock on Jupiter.

ALIEN 1: No rock on Jupiter? Do you hear that, Zak? They want some Jupiter rock.

ALIEN 2: So they can have some, right?

ALIENS: Yeah! Give me five! Right on!

*The* ALIENS *take up their position for another number.*

ALIEN 1: Because it just so happens that the current Number One in the Intergalactic charts is none other than . . .

ALIEN 2: Clock this one, kids!

ALIENS: Jupiter Rock!

MUSIC No. 13 — JUPITER ROCK

ALIENS (*sing*):

You can keep your rings of Saturn,
You can keep your moons of Mars.
You can keep your solar planets,
And your supernova stars,
Give me Jupiter Rock,
Give me Jupiter Rock,
You can keep the stars
Give me sixteen bars
Of Jupiter Rock.

You can keep your Solar System,
You can keep your Milky Way.
If there's one thing in the universe
That is really here to stay
It's Jupiter Rock,
It's Jupiter Rock.
You can keep the stars, give me sixteen bars
Of Jupiter Rock.

Jupiter — has to be the greatest,
Jupiter — it's the very latest,
Jupiter — it's the up-to-datest.
Jupiter, Jupiter Rock.

ALL (*sing*):

Take a sample for your spaceship,
It's the best thing of its kind.
It will energise your asteroids,
It will blow your cosmic mind.
Give me Jupiter Rock,
Give me Jupiter Rock.
You can keep the stars, give me sixteen bars
Of Jupiter Rock.

It will activate your motors,
It will make you go for bust.
It will get you into hyperdrive,
It will give your rocket thrust,
Give me Jupiter Rock,
Give me Jupiter Rock.
You can keep the stars,
Give me sixteen bars,
Of Jupiter Rock.
Jupiter Rock,
Jupiter Rock,
Jupiter Rock,
Jupiter Rock,
Yeah!

**Scene 4**

*The Secretary's office.* MRS TAYLOR *is resigned once more to an obscure position in life. There is a knock at the door and* MR CLAYTON *enters in the depths of gloom.*

MRS TAYLOR: Oh, hullo, Mr Clayton. Have you come to interview the superstar?

CLAYTON: Not really. Mind if I sit down?

MRS TAYLOR: Hey, what's the matter with you? You do look down in the dumps.

CLAYTON: I've been sacked. That's what.

MRS TAYLOR: Clayton of *The Clarion*?

CLAYTON: Sacked. Good as sacked anyway. My editor says I've made him the laughing stock of Fleet Street. I've got twenty four hours to come up with a scoop or else I'm fired.

MRS TAYLOR: Maybe something will turn up.

CLAYTON: In twenty four hours? Not in this place. We haven't had a story here in twenty four years.

MRS TAYLOR: Well, it might be managed.

CLAYTON: How do you mean?

MRS TAYLOR: Well, here we are at Mission Control. How about an exclusive interview with the Snodbury Space Crew?

CLAYTON: But they're not making contact for another week.

MRS TAYLOR: Oh, I just said that. Didn't take to those media people. Pushy lot.

CLAYTON: You mean you can still make contact.

MRS TAYLOR: Course I can. Watch this. Calling Starship Snodbury. This is Mission Control. Come in Starship Snodbury.

LINDA's *voice is heard offstage as if answering the radio.*

LINDA: Hullo, Mission Control. This is Starship Snodbury. Over.

MRS TAYLOR: Hullo, Linda. Where are you?

LINDA: Where are we? Let's see. Somewhere the other side of the Milky Way.

MRS TAYLOR: What are you doing up there?

LINDA: Looking for White Holes.

MRS TAYLOR: What for?

LINDA: We're going to put Mr Jones in one.

CLAYTON (*baffled*): They're going to put Mr Jones in one?

*The voices of the* CHILDREN *are heard singing.*

| | |
|---|---|
| CHILDREN *(sing)*: | *The Sauce, the Sauce, the Sauce for every course,*<br>*The Sauce will be with us always.* |
| CLAYTON: | What's all that about sauce? What's going on? |
| MRS TAYLOR: | Blowed if I know. Linda, what's all this sauce? (*Silence*) Oh bother. They've gone. Well, how about that, Mr Clayton? Is that any good? |
| CLAYTON: | Good? I'll say it's good. Take me to a typewriter. I've got a touch of the scoops coming on! |
| MRS TAYLOR: | That's the stuff. |
| CLAYTON (*starting to type*): | This could be the one, Mrs Taylor. This could be even better than your Susie. |

*Blackout.* MUSIC No. 14. *The band play one instrumental chorus of THE SAUCE IS WITH US while the crew take up their positions on the spaceship.*

**Scene 5**

*The* CHILDREN *are back on board the spaceship. They are all peering out of the windows, except for* GEORGE *and the* PROFESSOR *who are checking on a large gazeteer.*

| | |
|---|---|
| GEORGE: | Page 57 . . . square 4G. I'm sure we're right. |
| PROFESSOR: | Anyone see anything? |
| SALLY: | Not a sausage. |
| POLLY: | Hang on. What's that? Something's coming. |

*A* WHITE HOLE *appears.*

| | |
|---|---|
| WHITE HOLE: | Hullo there. |
| PROFESSOR: | Excuse me. Are you the White Hole? |
| WHITE HOLE: | Of course I am. What do I look like? |
| JIMMY: | We've made it. We've found one. |
| WHITE HOLE: | I should hope so. I've been waiting long enough. |
| PROFESSOR: | You knew we were coming? |
| WHITE HOLE: | Naturally. Out here news travels at light speed. You get tomorrow's headlines yesterday. Well, come on. Bring him out. Let's see what I can do. |
| POLLY: | Do you think it's dangerous. |
| SALLY: | I'm not sure. |
| WHITE HOLE: | No need to be frightened. I'm the Good Fairy. |
| PROFESSOR: | Who's going to take him out? Jimmy? |
| JIMMY: | No thanks. I've got no head for heights. How about you? |

PROFESSOR: I'm needed at the control desk. George?

GEORGE: I think the lunch needs looking at.

POLLY: How do we know it's friendly? It could be another Black Hole in disguise.

LINDA: Oh, come on. I'll do it. Pass Mr Jones.

LINDA *exits and approaches the* WHITE HOLE.

LINDA: Er, what do we do now?

WHITE HOLE: Give me Mr Jones.

LINDA: What's going to happen?

WHITE HOLE: Quite simple. I swallow him, and then he swells up.

LINDA: Back to normal size.

WHITE HOLE: That's it. Stand by.

LINDA *takes the tin inside the* WHITE HOLE's *voluminous costume and there is a terrific grunting and groaning.*

WHITE HOLE: Here he comes . . . (*Something incongruous like a large beachball emerges from under her costume.*) Is that him?

LINDA: No.

WHITE HOLE: Shucks. Let's have another go.

*There is more grunting and groaning. This time something else incongruous such as a piece of plastic drainpipe emerges.*

WHITE HOLE: How about that? (LINDA *shakes her head*) I knew it. It's going to be one of those days. (*To the band*) Come on. Give me a roll on the drums. I need all the help I can get . . . (*Roll on drums or tremolo or piano octaves*) Thank you. Now concentrate! Hey . . . Presto!

*This time, success. A bemused* MR JONES *emerges and starts to gabble incoherently.*

MR JONES: And speaking as the headmaster of Snodbury School, I have great pleasure in declaring this fete open . . . hey, where am I?

CHILDREN: In space!

MR JONES: What? Oh, yes. I had this strange dream — about being swallowed by a Black Hole.

PROFESSOR: That wasn't a dream, sir. And now you've been brought back to life by the White Hole.

MR JONES: I have? Er . . . how very kind of you.

WHITE HOLE: Not at all.

LINDA: Come on, sir. (*Leads* MR JONES *back into spaceship.*)

POLLY (*to* WHITE HOLE): You were fantastic!

JIMMY: Yeah! Really brilliant!

WHITE HOLE: All part of a day's work. I guess a White Hole's gotta do what a White Hole's gotta do. (*To Band*) Music, maestro!

*The* WHITE HOLE *sings a Reprise of THE BLACK HOLE SONG, but with different words:*

MUSIC No. 15 — THE WHITE HOLE SONG

WHITE HOLE (*sings*):

When you're shrunk in size,
Here's what I advise:
Find a White, White, White Hole.
That's what you must do
If it happens to you:
Find a White, White, White Hole.
Yes, a White Hole
Is the right hole,
It will get you out of any tight hole.
If your teacher's canned,
And needs to expand,
Find a White, White, White Hole.

If you're feeling small,
And want to walk tall,
Find a White, White, White Hole.
If you're keen to grow,
Then the person to know
Is a White, White, White Hole.
Yes, a White Hole
Is the right hole,
A restore-you-to-your-former-height hole.
If your teacher's canned
And needs to expand,
Find a White, White, White Hole.

(*Spoken*): Evening all. (*Exits*)

SALLY: Welcome back, sir.

MR JONES: Thank you. Thank you very much. How long have I been away?

JIMMY: Four weeks.

MR JONES: Four weeks! Well, there's no time to lose. We must get to Jupiter and collect the rock samples.

GEORGE: That's all right, Mr Jones. We've done all that.

MR JONES: You've done it? Incredible!

PROFESSOR: What do we do now, sir?

MR JONES: What do we do? I'll tell you what we do. We go home (*cheers from* CHILDREN). Get me Mission Control.

*Fade up lights on* MRS TAYLOR's *office to find* MR CLAYTON *typing,* DORIS *cleaning up and* MRS TAYLOR *filing. They stop when they hear* LINDA's *voice.*

LINDA: Hullo, Mission Control?

MRS TAYLOR: Oh, they're back.

LINDA: Starship Snodbury calling. Come in Mission Control.

MRS TAYLOR: Hullo there, Linda.

LINDA: Here's the Headmaster, Mrs Taylor.

MRS TAYLOR: Mr Jones?

DORIS: Is that 'im?

MRS TAYLOR: Think so.

DORIS: Ask 'im about the mops.

MRS TAYLOR: Hullo, Mr Jones. You've been awfully quiet. Everything gone all right?

MR JONES: Oh, fine. A little trouble with asteroid belts but apart from that, no problems.

MRS TAYLOR: I hear you've lost a bit of weight.

MR JONES: Well, I did. But now I've put it on again.

MRS TAYLOR: I'm sorry to hear that.

MR JONES: I'm not. Anyway, we're coming back, Mrs Taylor. Mission accomplished. We return home tomorrow afternoon.

MRS TAYLOR: Tomorrow afternoon?

DORIS *brandishes a mop in front of* MRS TAYLOR's *face who nods.*

MR JONES: That's right.

MRS TAYLOR: Fine, You'll just be in time for an appointment with the cleaning ladies.

MR JONES (*with bravado*): Cleaning ladies? What are cleaning ladies to a man who has been inside a Black Hole? Over and out.

*Fade out lights on spaceship.*

MRS TAYLOR: There you are then. Hot from the press. They're coming back tomorrow.

CLAYTON: And they're OK?

MRS TAYLOR: Yes. They're all fine apart from Mr Jones. What was it? (*Looks at her notes*) His asteroids have been playing him up.

CLAYTON: Great! That wraps it up then. Stand by . . . for a Clayton exclusive!

*He rips a sheet of paper from the typewriter and dashes out. Fade out lights on* MRS TAYLOR's *office. Fade up lights on spaceship.*

POLLY: Will we really be back tomorrow?

MR JONES: I don't see why not. (*Cheer from* CHILDREN) I thought you'd been having a good time.

GEORGE: Well, we have. But we still want to get back.

MR JONES: Don't you think it's beautiful up here?

SALLY: Not as beautiful as Earth.

LINDA: Anyway, I want to see my dog again.

PROFESSOR: I want a go on my micro.

JIMMY: And I want to watch Chelsea.

(*Short silence*)

MR JONES: Time to go home then?

ALL: Yes, sir. Time to go home.

MUSIC No. 16 — TAKE ME HOME

SPACE CREW (*sing*):

Take me home,
I'm tired of the stars.
Take me home,
I'm fed up with Mars.
Take me home.
I somehow know
It's time to go
Back home.

Out in space
Our starship has flown
Far away
To places unknown.
Now it's time
To say goodbye.
Say goodbye,
It's time to fly
Back home.

Earth is home,
Nowhere else will do.
Earth is home,
Home for me and you.
Earth is home,
That's the place to be.
Earth is home
For you and me.

Take me home,
It's time to go back.
Out in space,
The outlook is black.
Take me home,
I'm tired of space.
Out is space
Is not the place
For me.

Take me home,
I'm tired of the stars.
Take me home,
I'm fed up with Mars.
Take me home.
I somehow know,
I just know
It's time to go
Back home.

*The Secretary's office.* MRS TAYLOR *is pinning up a large notice saying 'Welcome home, Mr Jones'.* MR CLAYTON *rushes in.*

MRS TAYLOR: Oh, hullo.

CLAYTON: Guess what! I've got my job back.

MRS TAYLOR: Oh lovely! What did he say?

CLAYTON: "Mr Clayton, my confidence in you has never wavered. Your article is in the finest traditions of British journalism." Salary doubled!

MRS TAYLOR: Good for you!

CLAYTON: Judgement and experience, Mrs Taylor (*taps nose*). Priceless commodities.

MISS HUGGINS *come storming in.*

MISS HUGGINS: Well, when are they due?

MRS TAYLOR (*frostily*): Ah, Miss Huggins.

MISS HUGGINS: Estimated time of arrival, please.

MRS TAYLOR: In about half an hour, I think. Have you come to welcome them back.

MISS HUGGINS: Hardly that. Mr Jones has driven a coach and horses through the borough regulations. He is clearly incapable of running a fish and chip shop, let alone a school. It will give me considerable pleasure to inform the press outside that Snodbury School is being closed down.

MRS TAYLOR: What! You can't close it down. Mr Jones is famous!

MISS HUGGINS: Mr Jones is not paid to be a celebrity. He's a headmaster, not Yuri Gagarin.

MRS TAYLOR: But what's he done wrong?

MISS HUGGINS: Regulation 147: "Schools wishing to make an excursion more than ten miles from the school premises must first secure permission from County Hall." Did he write to County Hall? No, he did not. Regulation 375, para 32, subsection F: "School parties must at all times travel in authorised school buses."

*The telephone rings.*

MRS TAYLOR: Snodbury Middle School . . . Who did you say that was? 10 Downing Street . . . certainly I'll hang on. (*Puts hand over phone briefly.*) Oh, Miss Huggins, I don't know if you know Mr Clayton. He's from *The Clarion.* (*Resumes conversation on phone.*) Yes, certainly I'll pass on your best wishes. (*She starts to relay the conversation to* CLAYTON.) "And congratulations to the far-sighted local authority for supporting such a venture . . . Mr Jones and the borough are an example to Great Britain . . . Long may they continue to work in harness." Thank you very much, Ma'am. (*Replaces receiver*) Well!!

CLAYTON: Extremely interesting, Miss Huggins. In view of the Prime Minister's comments, I wonder if you'd care to let our readers know how the borough will be viewing the future of Snodbury School.

MISS HUGGINS: Well . . . er . . . in the light of overall circumstances, we can perhaps take a lenient view of some technical misdemeanours.

CLAYTON: I see the Press are arriving. Will you be speaking to them about the future of the school?

MISS HUGGINS: Er . . . naturally . . . yes, of course. We have our reputation to bear in mind.

CLAYTON (*consulting notes*): What was it? Far-sighted local authority?

MISS HUGGINS: Very far-sighted. Long may we continue to work in harness.

MISS HUGGINS *exits to make a statement to the Press.*

CLAYTON: Was that really the Prime Minister?

MRS TAYLOR: Prime Minister? Oh, dear me, no! That was my friend Doris.

CLAYTON: What!

MRS TAYLOR: Yes, I told her to give me a ring when Miss Huggins arrived. Let's see what she's got to say now.

*They join the Press Conference outside.*

MISS HUGGINS: To avoid any misunderstanding, I should like to put on record that the Space Mission has had the full backing of the Education Committee. Snodbury Middle School is the jewel in our educational crown.

1ST REPORTER: What about the plans to close it down?

MISS HUGGINS: A ludicrous rumour. This is an outstanding school with an outstanding headmaster. Its future is guaranteed.

MRS TAYLOR: Hey! They're coming! They're coming!

MISS HUGGINS: In view of our reputation as a far-sighted authority . . .

1ST REPORTER: Mind your back, lady.

MISS HUGGINS *is pushed to one side as* THE MEDIA *switch their attention to the back of the hall.* GLADYS, MAVIS *and* DORIS *emerge. They are holding a banner attached to their mops which reads 'WELCOME BACK, STARSHIP SNODBURY'.*

GLADYS, MAVIS *and* DORIS 2 . . . 4 . . . 6 . . . 8 . . . Who do we appreciate?
S . . . N . . . O . . . D . . . B . . . U . . . R . . . Y . . .
Snodbury!

TV MAN (*holding a mike and facing camera*): Are we running? Turn over . . . And so this historic space journey comes to an end as Starship Snodbury glides down to earth for a perfect touchdown. Eat your heart out, Neil Armstrong. The space heroes of today are Snodbury

Middle School and their intrepid commander, Astronaut Jones. (*Cheers from* ALL *on stage*) And even as I speak, Starship Snodbury has landed. We have touchdown! The door opens and out they come.

THE CREW *enter the back of the hall and advance to the stage surrounded by other Snodbury pupils.*

MUSIC No. 17 — RULE BRITANNIA *is played to wild cheering.*

MRS TAYLOR: Hullo, Mr Jones. Welcome back, children.

DORIS (*placing wreath round his neck*): Our hero! We think you're fabulous, Mr Jones. Isn't that right, girls?

MAVIS *and* GLADYS: Definitely fabulous.

MRS TAYLOR: And Miss Huggins thinks you're fabulous as well.

MR JONES (*astonished*): What!

MRS TAYLOR: The school is saved!

MISS HUGGINS: Naturally. You know you've always had our complete support.

DORIS: What about the mops?

MISS HUGGINS: They have our complete support too. New mops all round.

2ND REPORTER: How does it feel to be back, Headmaster?

MR JONES: How does it feel? I would say over the moon.

CHILDREN: Over the moon. Definitely. Over the moon.

3RD REPORTER: And how was the flight? Can you describe the trip?

MR JONES: Certainly. It was one small Middle for Snodbury Step School . . . It was one giant Middle for mankind. Oh, drat it!

LINDA: Leave it to us, sir. We'll tell them.

MUSIC No. 18 — LET'S GO TO THE PLANETS

SPACE CREW *(sing)*:

We've been to the planets,
We've been to the stars.
We've journeyed to Jupiter,
We've journeyed to Mars.
We've been to the universe
To search and explore,
Where a thousand stars were waiting,
A thousand stars and more.

ALL:

Sail through the heavens,
Through the universe wide,
Where the planets turn
And the meteors burn,
And the Milky Way shines bright.
Sail through the heavens,
Through the universe wide,

We have journeyed far,
With the brightest star
As our beacon and our guide.

They've been to the planets,
They've been to the stars.
They've journeyed to Jupiter,
They've journeyed to Mars.
They've been to the universe,
To search and explore,
Where a thousand stars were waiting,
A thousand stars and more.

*A* TELEX OFFICIAL *comes running in from the back of the hall.*

TELEX OFFICIAL: Telexes for Mr Jones. Urgent telexes.

MRS TAYLOR: Who from?

MR JONES: Let's see. (*Reads telex*) "White House to Snodbury. Zowie! Suggest ticker-tape parade soonest. Ring to confirm details."

TELEX OFFICIAL: This one's from Moscow.

MR JONES: "Congratulations to Comrade Jones, on bold fight against Crypto-Fascist Education Committees."

TELEX OFFICIAL: The last one's from outer space. A Mr Uffo?

MR JONES: Let me see. "Congratulations, Mr Jones . . . Have decided to take your name. Stop. Identity crisis solved. Signed: U.F.O. Jones. PS. Congratulations to the band as well. They accompanied me very nicely. (*The cast lead the applause for the band*) PPS. Was so impressed by everyone that I will be visiting your school shortly in person."

UFO *rushes in from the back.*

UFO: And here I am, a little earlier than expected because I bring urgent news. I hate to spoil the party but I feel you ought to know that the Black Hole has just entered the Hall. (*The cast lead the boos as the* BLACK HOLE *appears*) But all is not lost because the White Hole has also arrived.

*The cast lead the cheers as the* WHITE HOLE *appears down the other aisle.*

*As the* BLACK HOLE *and* WHITE HOLE *advance down different aisles, they sing a verse of their songs simultaneously.*

MUSIC No. 19 — THE BLACK HOLE SONG *and* THE WHITE HOLE SONG (*Reprise*)

*The* BLACK HOLE *and the* WHITE HOLE *sing simultaneously.*

BLACK HOLE (*sings*):

I'm black as night,
I squeeze you tight,
I'm the Black, Black, Black Hole.
I squeeze you flat
To the size of a gnat,
I'm the Black, Black, Black Hole.
I can seize you,
I can squeeze you,
In a way that's not designed to please you.
You'll disappear,
If you come too near
To a Black, Black, Black Hole.

WHITE HOLE (*sings*):

When you're shrunk in size,
Here's what I advise,
Find a White, White, White Hole.
That's what you must do,
If it happens to you,
Find a White, White, White Hole.
Yes, a White Hole
Is the right hole.
It will get you out of any tight hole.
If your teacher's canned,
And he needs to expand,
Find a White, White, White Hole.

*The* WHITE HOLE *points her wand at the* BLACK HOLE *at the end of the song.*

WHITE HOLE: In the name of Mr Jones, I command you to vanish.

(*The* BLACK HOLE *collapses to the ground in a heap of black cloth.*)

2ND REPORTER: What was the scientific objective of the mission, Mr Jones?

MR JONES: To find some Jupiter rock.

3RD REPORTER: But there isn't any on Jupiter.

MR JONES: No rock on Jupiter? You want some Jupiter rock? (*Cast shouts "YES"*) You shall have it!

MUSIC No. 20 — JUPITER ROCK (*Reprise*)

ALL (*sing*):

You can keep your rings of Saturn,
You can keep your moons of Mars.
You can keep your solar planets,
And your supernova stars,
Give me Jupiter Rock,
Give me Jupiter Rock,
You can keep the stars
Give me sixteen bars
Of Jupiter Rock.

You can keep your Solar System,
You can keep your Milky Way.
If there's one thing in the universe
That is really here to stay
It's the Jupiter Rock,
It's the Jupiter Rock.
You can keep the stars, give me sixteen bars
Of Jupiter Rock.

Jupiter — has to be the greatest,
Jupiter — it's the very latest,
Jupiter — it's the up-to-datest.
Jupiter, Jupiter Rock!
Jupiter — everybody try it!
Jupiter — everybody buy it!
All the best record shops supply it.
Jupiter, Jupiter Rock!

Take a sample for your spaceship,
It's the best thing of its kind.
It will energise your asteroids,
It will blow your cosmic mind.
Give me Jupiter Rock,
Give me Jupiter Rock.
You can keep the stars, give me sixteen bars
Of Jupiter Rock.
Jupiter Rock,
Jupiter Rock,
Jupiter Rock,
Jupiter Rock,
Yeah!

(CURTAIN)





Printed by Watkiss Studios Ltd., Biggleswade, Beds. 01/98